Woman More Than Just a Rib

Woman
More Than Just
a Rib

Janie C. Williams

© 2006 by Janie C. Williams. All rights reserved.

Printed in the United States of America

No part of this publication may be reproduced, stored in a retrieval system, or transmitted in any way by any means—electronic, mechanical, photocopy, recording, or otherwise—without the prior permission of the copyright holder, except as provided by USA copyright law.

Scriptures references are taken from the King James Version of the Bible.

Ufomadu Consulting & Publishing (UC&P)
P.O. Box 746
Selma, AL 36702-0746
www.UfomaduConsulting.com

ISBN 0-9754197-8-1
Library of Congress Catalog Card Number: 2006902534

In Memoriam
November 15, 1917 - March 4, 2002

Lizzie Cox Coleman, my mother, for instilling in me godly precepts; not only with words, but by example also. A godly "more than" woman indeed, who left behind a godly legacy for her family.

Dedication

This book is dedicated to:

Renee and Regina, my daughters, who inspire me and love me for being just who I am, myself. They are intelligent more than women.

Robert (Robbie), my son, who keeps me smiling with his playful ways. My supporter.

Evie Gamble, my friend and confidant, who knows my flaws and faults but loves me anyhow. A humble more than woman.

My niece, Linda Jowers, who has always been there for me when I needed her. Only God knows how much I love you Linda.

Carrie Cox, my "listener" from way back when. Keep on keeping on.

Mary Thigpen, a woman to be admired for her honesty and encouragement. My friend.

Cynthia Adams, my shero that knows how to make a difference that counts. Cynthia, the Body of Christ is waiting for you. Hurry!

Phyllis Woods, a young woman with a bright future. Thanks for the many prayers on my behalf. God received them.

Elder Elvin Woods, the man of God yet to be discovered. The divine ladder of God awaits you, start climbing. Success is yours.

Frankie Allen, a grand more than woman. So humble, so sweet, so wise, so godly. You are truly an inspiration to other women.

Elder Jimmy Allen, thanks for believing in me. Continue to be the man of God that you are.

Gustavia Coleman, the "mouth" in the family. Keep talking, because if you should stop, I will know to take you to *a doctor immediately. Thanks for everything you have done for me.*

Robert Williams, Sr., my husband, the motivation that help to birth this book. You help me to realize that I am truly a more than woman. A million thanks to you.

Tyrenee, my sunshine, my buttercup, my granddaughter; the gift God gave me as a comfort after my mother went to heaven. A delight to my life. A future more than woman for sure.

Table of Contents

Introduction		11
Ch. 1	The Power of Influence	15
Ch. 2	Beautiful, Built, Bold	21
Ch. 3	I Am More Than That	25
Ch. 4	A Woman of Perseverance	33
Ch. 5	You Have a Future	37
Ch. 6	Just Do It	43
Ch. 7	Classy and Courageous	51
Ch. 8	Shameful Past—Shining Future	59
Ch. 9	Divine Persistence for a Divine Destiny	69
Ch. 10	Betters Days Ahead	79
Ch. 11	The Essence of True Womanhood	81

Introduction

  I am a builder of womanhood. I am an exhorter of good moral character and outstanding qualities for women. We cannot and we must not see ourselves as just a rib. Let me tell you why. When a woman sees herself as just a rib, she views herself unworthy and undeserving of life's best. She sees herself as merely this, or barely that, and nothing more.

  The American College Dictionary defines rib as "a long, slender, curved bone. A piece of meat (flesh)." Rib is also defined as "a structured well-put together member that is used for strength and support; and in joking terms, rib means a wife."

  Indeed, some women are long, slender, and curvy. We are indeed structured and well-put together. We provide strength and support; yet we are a lot more. Skillfully and purposely, God made woman to be more than just a rib. The bone that God pulled out of Adam's side was bare and lacking. There was no life in it. It was lacking physically, mentally, emotionally, and spiritually. It was only a rib. Bare and lifeless, it had no potential like it was, and no capabilities. It could not think, speak, move, make decisions, or anything else. There was no power in that rib whatsoever. It was only a bone taken out of Adam until God constructed His masterpiece. Get this: the rib in itself was not God's masterpiece, the woman He created from that rib was His masterpiece. The word masterpiece means, "One's most excellent production." Woman was God's most excellent production. Out of all the things He created and called into existence, woman stood out more than anything else.

  After God finished molding that rib, He had designed it into a woman, complete and whole. It was at that particular moment that the rib became "more than." Fact is, God had fashioned something great and unique. That rib was no longer just a bone because it had become of much greater importance. In addition to the outer things—head, face, eyes, hands, feet, etc., there were the inner things. There was the mind, heart, soul, spirit, and will. There was inner beauty as well as outer beauty. That rib had become a woman, namely, Eve.

In writing this book, I want to exhort every woman to see yourself as God sees you. See yourself as He created you to be—whole and complete, with inner and outer beauty. See yourself through the eyes of God, for then and only then will you be able to feel secure in your womanhood.

*Jesus said, "**Occupy until I come**." (See Luke 19:13) I encourage and challenge women everywhere to do exactly that. Occupy your seat and your position of womanhood until Jesus returns.*

And the Lord God said, it is not good that the man should be alone; I will make him an helpmeet for him.

And out of the ground the Lord God formed every beast of the field, and every fowl of the air, and brought them unto Adam to see what he would call them: and whatsoever Adam called every living creature, that was the name thereof.

And Adam gave names to all cattle, and to the fowl of the air, and to every beast of the field; but for Adam there was not found an helpmeet for him.

And the Lord God caused a deep sleep to fall upon Adam, and he slept: and he took one of his ribs, and closed up the flesh thereof;

And the rib, which the Lord God had taken from man, made he a woman, and brought her unto the man.

And Adam said, This is now bone of my bones, and flesh of my flesh: she shall be called woman, because she was taken out of man.

Genesis 2:18-23

The Power of Influence

Every woman has the power to influence. We have the ability to generate changes through our words, actions, behaviors, and conduct. We have the power to impel, move, and sway others. A woman can motivate, spur, inspire, and incite, or she can hinder, hamper, impede, and obstruct. Therefore, our power to influence can be used for good or bad. Consequently, we must be careful how we use it.

Eve was Adam's helpmeet. She was his bride, companion, lover, partner, and wife. She was his sweetheart, his squeeze, his woman. She was suitable, appropriate, becoming, and complementary to him, as well as for him. As a result, she enhanced Adam.

When God presented Eve to Adam, He presented a complete woman. Eve was beautiful, meticulously formed, exciting to look upon, and she was comforting and soothing to Adam's touch. Eve had a mind that was sharp, clever, and thirsty for knowledge. Her Maker had created her to be more than just a rib.

There was more to her than just a pretty face. She was more than a shapely body, and she was more than a beautiful glossy head of hair. Her mouth was more than something to be kissed, and she was more than something to touch, caress, and fondle. She was not just sensual and sexy, but she was also smart and intelligent.

Furthermore, Eve was a woman with great inner qualities and inner beauty. Having a mind, soul, heart, spirit, and will, she possessed her own identity—she was woman! Adam did not call her Mrs. Adam; he called her woman. Having Mrs. in front of your name does not give you your identity.

Allow me to point out this fact: Eve was there inside Adam all the time waiting to be taken out and given an identity. Here is the evidence.

"Male and female created he them...and called their name Adam." Genesis 5:2. Woman was not, I repeat, not, an afterthought of God. She was not a spur of the moment thing or decision. God purposely made them one flesh and gave them one name signifying that there should be unity and oneness between husband and wife.

Designed to be a woman of vital importance, Eve was good for Adam spiritually, intellectually, socially, and physically. She was intended to give love, and she was created to be loved. Woman was and still is U-M-M-M, good. In addition, God fashioned Eve to be adaptable to Adam's needs. She was divinely endowed to be whatever Adam needed her to be to him to the best of her ability without demeaning herself, or disrespecting herself.

When God fashioned Eve to be adaptable, He proved beyond a shadow of doubt that He made woman to be more than just a rib. Eve came fully equipped with everything she needed as a woman because she had more than one function to perform. Keep in mind that Eve was a vessel of adaptability to Adam, not a vessel to be broken, crushed, or abused by him.

Eve's face, form, and features were God's choice. Fortunately, Adam had no say or input in the designing of Eve. Still, he was highly pleased and impressed with Eve because his reaction was: bone of my bone, flesh of my flesh, this shall be called Woman, for from me was she taken. Adam implies, I, man, am somebody; so woman taken out of me is somebody, too. I concur with that inference. In any case, God created woman with grace, dignity, stability, intelligence, beauty, and influence. Thanks to her Creator, woman came into her own. She did not come needy. Man, namely Adam, was the needy one. "...[B]ut for Adam there was not found an helpmeet for him." Woman was and still is a multifarious powerhouse of characteristics. She possesses a great variety of talents, abilities, and skills.

Since Eve, all women are endowed and equipped by their Creator when they are born. We simply need to grow and mature into adulthood. However, we can still enhance ourselves in many ways. We are to excel in our endeavors while intelligently understanding and accepting that sometimes we can and will fail. Learn from the failure and move on. The ability to do so is there within us. We may be satin on the outside, but we, however, can be steel on the inside; meaning, we have the capacity to be strong and determined internally.

Ladies, get beyond seeing yourself the way modern magazines define women. Get beyond seeing yourself as a piece of flesh whose sole purpose is to provide sexual pleasure for a man. You are more than some man's sex toy. See yourself as having more than just a sex drive. Move beyond being just a glamorous airhead. God created you smart and intelligent.

There is more to being a woman than having on the right shade of lipstick, the right make-up, or having just the right hair style. You are more than a fashion statement. Lots more! As a woman, you are more than 42 ways to sexual pleasure, and more than just knowing how to do 66 things to a naked man. When a woman reads statements in magazines such as these, she should be incensed because it is thinking of this nature that helps to debase womanhood. Statements such as these reduce the quality and value of womanhood. This way of thinking lowers, corrupts, defiles, degrades, and perverts the very honor of womanhood.

Enrich yourself, not just financially, but spiritually and intellectually, as well. Know how to do more than firm your butt and rock some man's world. Learn how to use your hands on more than just his body. A real woman should want to know more than what turns a man on at ages twenty-five, thirty-five, and forty-five. Endeavor to learn more than twenty-three ways to make a man insane with desire. Learn how to soar with your talents, gifts, and abilities in a manner that will bring glory to God and impact lives.

Women, work at having more than a firm tummy, tush, and thighs. Sure, look good and exercise, but see yourself as more than the slimmest, sexiest body around. You are more than just a woman with great breasts and sexy, shapely legs. Empower yourself! God made you to be more than a pleasure zone for some man. In life you should want to achieve more than hassle-free hair and pretty skin.

Altogether too many women allow television, movies, and popular magazines to reduce and diminish them to being just a rib. According to their way of viewing life, everything is physical. Let me tell you something exciting—God created woman to be more, more, more! He created woman to be greater than her outward appearance. God created you to do notable and praiseworthy things, to go places, and to make a worthwhile difference in this world. You have thinking power, talking power, and action power. You have the power to influence and inflame. You have the power of prayer, praise, and performance. Realize you are more than a piece of curvaceous flesh; you are a powerhouse of creativity.

Prepare yourself; do not get stuck--your "afterperiod" is coming! *After* that shapely figure is gone; *after* your face is no longer breath-takingly beautiful; *after* the glossy hair starts turning grey; *after* that man is no longer interested in holding your hand, kissing your lips, or holding you close; *after* he no longer wants to run his fingers through your hair; and *after* he no longer wants to touch, caress, or fondle you, what then?

Now you can see why it is so important that you see yourself as more than just a rib; to see yourself as God sees you.

God gave you, woman, worth. Being a helpmeet is only part of that God-given worth. Woman is courageous as well as caressable; devoted, as she is desirable; smart, not just sensual and sexy; prayerful, as well as pretty; and talented, as she is touchable. So stop waiting around hoping for something to just fall into your life. Stop saying, "I wish," instead, say, "With God's help, I can and I will."

The same God who created Oprah Winfrey, Hillary Clinton, Maya Angelou, Maxine Brown, Mother Teresa, and Johnetta B. Cole created you. Do you know who Johnetta B. Cole is, by any chance? Let me tell you. She is a former president of Spelman College. Ms. Cole coined the term *shero*. There are three definitions given for the word shero. My favorite is: "A woman admired for her achievements, wisdom, and noble qualities."

Johnetta B. Cole is a shero, indeed. She is a woman who puts her thinking power into action; a woman who utilizes both her speaking power and action power. She is a woman that uses her power to influence and impact minds.

Absorb this, God created you to be a sheroic woman, also. He created you to achieve, excel, and influence. You might say to yourself, "I'm not sure about that." Well, God made you woman, didn't He? Therefore, you must continue dreaming that seemingly impossible dream. There is a God who delights in doing the so-called impossible things. Keep reaching for those supposedly unreachable stars, namely, those goals that seem beyond your grasp.

That certain desire of your heart that will not manifest itself, keep believing and expecting it to happen. Know this, it is in God that you live, move, and have your being. All things can be accomplished through Him when they meet His approval.

Remember, you are more than a rib; you are a powerhouse of influence.

Beautiful, Built, Bold

Wanted: A woman who's beautiful, built, and bold. If this ad appeared in a newspaper, I can assure you there will be hundreds, if not thousands of responses. Indeed, there are many beautiful, bold, and well-built women in the world today. The question to ask however, is whether or not this is the essentiality of womanhood?

Vashti was such a woman, but she was more than just a beautiful, bold woman with a nice figure. From the start, she knew she was more than just a rib (see Esther 1:10-21). Her impressive beauty was also characterized by modesty and respect for herself. This lady recognized that she was woman before she was wife or queen. Summoned by King Ahasuerus, she boldly made her decision to refuse his drunken request.

How easy it is for some men to look upon women as mere physical objects. Ahasuerus seemed to be such a man. For him, his wife was something to be gazed at solely for physical purposes. He treated Vashti as a mere possession, not like the wonderful, respectable woman God created and ordained her to be. He saw his wife as only a rib.

Modesty and respectability should not be abandoned because a woman gains a title or position. Before title or position, she is still woman. Her title or position does not make her what she already is.

Ahasuerus' focus was on Vashti's physical charms only. He could not seem to get past her beautiful face and great body. This is why being beautiful, built, and bold must not be the essentiality of womanhood. For if it was, there are many women who would not meet this criterion. Thankfully, womanhood is not based on whether or not a woman is these three things.

Do not misunderstand me, there is nothing wrong with a man focusing on a woman's physical charms, unless he fails to realize there is more to a woman than her outer attractions. All too often, women are used by some men for only a pleasurable delight and thrill. These men treat women shabbily and disgracefully.

God forbid if a woman's only purpose in life is to satisfy a man's sexual needs. As his wife, this is just one of her duties and delights. However, there is more, a great deal more to a woman than her sexuality. A man cheats himself when his focus is sexual only. He misses out on so many wonderful and exciting things with a woman when his focus is warped.

Refusing to cater to her husband's drunken vanity was an admirable quality in Vashti, true enough; but unfortunately, Vashti had not prepared herself for the hour of crisis. She reacted to her husband's request without praying about it first. This was a big mistake. Actions minus prayer invite disaster. In a crisis, a quickly whispered prayer is better than no prayer. God hears this kind of prayer, as well as the long, wordy prayer when it is prayed in sincerity.

Vashti's error was not taking a stand for herself, but the error was the way, manner, and attitude in which she took her stand. Although Ahasuerus' focus was warped, he was still the voice of authority in the palace because he was the king. A woman should respect the voice of authority, even if she refuses to act on the command given. In other words, honor the office; never blatantly disregard protocol.

There will be times when we as women will have to deal with warped voices of authority. Ladies, use wisdom and deal wisely. There is a way out of any situation, but there is a wrong way out and a right way out.

Unfortunately, Ahasuerus disgraced his wife in her position as queen and in her role as wife. He reduced her to being nothing more than a physical attraction for other men to ogle. Yet, somehow, Vashti stood strong in her womanly self-respect. As punishment, she was banished from her position as queen and her role as Ahasuerus' wife.

Still, she left knowing for herself that she was more than just a rib. She lost her crown as queen, but maintained her dignity, and retained her crown of exalted womanhood. Although she lost her title, she walked away with her self-respect in tact. Sometimes you have to lose in order to win. Vashti walked away a winner, and she scored one for womanhood.

Women, please know that you are more than a beautiful face and a well-built body. God never intended for women to be treated shabbily or disgracefully. Yet there are women that allow themselves to be treated this way for the sake of having a man in their lives. Womanhood should be esteemed highly. Women should be shining pictures of feminine respectability, yet strong in the divine power of almighty God.

Purposely be determined, while still maintaining your dignity. Be humble in spirit, but boldly exalt that which is good and pure. Sometimes a woman can know that she is more than just a rib and still be powerless to do anything about her bad situation in her own strength. If you are in an abusive situation, allow God to intervene on your behalf. Knowing what to do and being able to do it are two different things.

Therefore, you should allow God to empower and equip you to deal wisely with your situation. Call upon His grace and power. Prayer can transform a defeated woman into a determined, courageous one. Using wisdom, sort out your situation. Be a woman of clear judgment and self-control, as well as a woman of fasting and prayer. Some things will not happen by prayer only. You must combine your prayers with fasting and faith to obtain the results you need.

When exalted, womanhood can be stars of hope, joy, and inspiration to other women who find themselves depending on their beauty and body to get them through life.

In today's society, there are many factors that undermine true womanhood. We are not to fall for these things or perceive them as the in-thing to do. They are not! They serve only to debase and reduce womanhood; to make it less than what God intended for women.

Too often, women allow their bodies to be put on display in magazines and movies scenes for all the world to see. These Hollywood-style antics only pull women further and further into disrespect and disgrace. This is justified by saying that the body is a thing of beauty and women should not be ashamed of their bodies. The fact is, they are right on both accounts. The body is a beautiful thing, and women should not be ashamed of their bodies.

"For I am fearfully and wonderfully made, marvelous are thy works..." Psalms 139:14. As you can see, even Scripture attests to this truth that the body is a beautiful work of God and not to be viewed as something embarrassing. However, the body is also a very private thing, not to be put on display for others to gaze upon. Only in the privacy of one's home or other private enclosures, and only for the pleasure and enjoyment of one's spouse--and him alone should a woman's body be utilized.

Vashti knew this. She did not fall for the misguided, warped flattery from Ahasuerus. How easy it is to fall for those things that only bring humiliation and scandal upon one's life. Refuse to be a victim or prey for things of this nature. Instead, go for the greater and honorable things God has prepared for you as a woman in this morally corrupt world.

I Am More Than That

Life does not always turn out the way we imagined that it would. During our teenage years, we fantasized about being happily married to a handsome man who would treat us like queens. For many of us, however, this fantasy remained just that, a fantasy. We got married, but unfortunately, the marriage and the relationship turned acrimonious.

There are many reasons why a marital relationship turns bitter; the chief reason is that Satan, the thief of all good things, sabotages the relationship.

Meet the woman of Samaria. (See St. John 4). Driven by loneliness and emptiness, she repeats the same destructive behavior patterns again and again. Instead of judging her though, let us apply our hearts and minds to understand her inappropriate behavior and lifestyle.

First of all, she had a legitimate need, but kept trying to fill that need the wrong way. Repeatedly, she tried to fill an inner need using external means, namely men. And that was the problem—she kept filling the need.

These men were like clouds without water. They promised much, but produced nothing. They were broken cisterns that were unable to quench her thirst, or fill her emptiness. She, on the other hand, being a wandering star, kept moving from man to man. She did not know how to value herself enough to take stock of her life and realize that she was being used.

These men did not have the power or ability to provide her with what she really needed. Yet, they took advantage of the fact that she was lonely and wanted to be loved. She was their victim, as well as their prey. This poor, empty, lonely woman was well-known in the city by the men for one reason, and well-known by the women for another reason. In fact, she wore many labels. She was labeled a homewrecker, husband stealer, and promiscuous. Moving from one crummy relationship to another, she kept seeking after something, but what, she did not really know. In turn, she became the neighborhood's outcast.

Having the reputation that she did, other women avoided her because of her lack of respectability, and because they saw her as a threat to them and their homes. The men saw her as an easy mark; and she saw herself as unworthy of anything good. Already married five times before, she was now living with another woman's husband.

Here we have another woman who saw herself as just a rib. Subsequently, she did not view herself important enough to wait for the love of a good man. Her situation being as it was, she became discontented in life and with life. Men came and went in her life. You will never keep anything that is not rightfully yours without suffering the consequences. Besides, sooner or later, the vanishing act takes place. Now you have it, now you don't.

Actually, this woman needed a genuine friend. She thought it was sex that she needed, but it was not about sex, as she later found out. Of course, the men in her life were not about to tell her that; they had a good thing going for themselves. The wrong kind of people in your life will feed your low self-esteem and insecurities.

Fortunately for this woman, during the course of her destructive lifestyle, she encountered One who knew how to deal with every need effectively. *"If thou knewest the gift of God,"* she was told. Sex is a gift from God to be enjoyed within the confines of marriage. However, this woman was using the wrong gift to take the place of the right gift. How tragic that so many women will often try to fill a legitimate need with the wrong gift. Absolutely too many women go to the wrong sources for what they need, as this woman did.

Finally, after five failed relationships, she met the One who had the real power and ability to supply her real need. She met One who knew how to give her the desires of her heart that were good for her; she met Jesus. He saw her as a worthy human being that needed His help. Jesus knew something she had not realized yet. He knew that she was more than what men saw her as, and He knew she was more than the labels that were pinned on her by the people in Samaria. Jesus knew she was more than just a rib.

Not only that, Jesus knew she was more than a piece of flesh to be fondled, touched, or caressed. She was more than a topic of conversation for the gossipers. Jesus looked beyond all that stuff and saw substance. That's why it was necessary for Him to go to Samaria. Wherever there is a need, Jesus is there. Do not ever doubt this truth. Not only is He there, but He is there to do something about the need.

At first, this woman was suspicious of Jesus' intentions towards her. Suspiciously, she asks, *"How is it that you being a Jew are asking me, a Samaritan, for a drink of water, knowing that the Jews and the Samaritans have no dealings with each other?"*

One must understand that she was used to men approaching her with ulterior motives. Jesus, however, was not just another man. He was not there to use her. He was there to help her recognize the real need she had in her life. This awesome Man was there to let her know that His grace was greater than her disgrace; and His forgiveness greater than her faults. His mission was to awaken her to a new and better life for herself.

There were no strings attached, no deals made, and no extraction of a promise from her to meet Him after dark. To put it plainly, she did not have to go to bed with Him to attain that better life.

Accepting Jesus' offer, her response was, *"Sir, give me this water* [. . .]" She was thirsty; she was ready for a change, and she received it.

For many women, it is time to realize something—with only sex in your life, you will thirst again, for sex is only a temporary solution. Sex will never satisfy your spiritual need. The above-mentioned woman of Samaria had many men in her life, but time after time, they left her thirsty. Man will never take the place of Christ in a woman's life because there are some needs a man just cannot fill. How can that which is temporal, finite, and flawed, take the place of One who is eternal, infinite, and perfect? Yet, man has a place in woman's life. His designated, divinely, ordained place, that is.

If you are in this type of situation, allow your eyes to become open like this woman did. It finally dawned on her that Jesus was a different kind of man. This woman, confused and lonely, had found a mighty good man in Jesus. As a result, she now had something to tell all the men in the city. So off she went to find the so-called men; men whose focus was only on the physical attractions of women, and she tells them—*"Come see a man [. . .]"*.

A man—a man who is different from all of you; a man who is superior and above all men in His thinking and concepts toward women; a man who told me how to get up instead of pulling me down, One that put self-worth and self-esteem within me; a man who knows how to treat a lady like a lady, even when she has been labeled and not acting like a lady.

What a man indeed! Jesus took a woman who saw herself as nothing—a nobody—and convinced her that she was worthy to be something and somebody. Naturally, when she left Jesus and went her way, she went knowing that she was more than just a rib.

Indeed, knowledge is power, and Jesus armed this lonely, confused, and needy woman with powerful knowledge. At last, she had the knowledge that Jesus could and would be far more significant in her life than twenty men ever could. In addition, Jesus armed her with the awareness that with Him, she did not have to lower her morals, or her principles for His love. Jesus proves by His actions toward this woman that He is a builder of womanhood.

Women, allow nothing and no one to deceive you into seeing yourself as nothing through your own eyes. See yourself as God sees you. He sees you as something special, wonderful, and unique. Also, know that sex will never take the place of the Savior in your life. Don't be a "piece" for some man to drop by and get whenever the whim hits him. When he tells his friends that he is about to go and get him a "piece," don't be the "piece" that he is referring to. You are a whole person. A man should know it is all, or nothing at all. Marriage is still honorable and the marriage bed is yet clean and undefiled.

Wherever you are today, and regardless of the situation that you are in right now, Jesus knows exactly where you are.

"*And He must needs go through Samaria.*" Just as Jesus knew this woman was in Samaria, He knows where you are located, also. He knows where your house is, the street and the number, as well as the city and the state. He also knows the location of the office, factory, company, or classroom where you are working.

If you are out on a limb, He knows that, too.

"*And Jesus entered and passed through Jericho.*

And, behold, there was a man name Zacchaeus, which was the chief among the publicans, and he was rich.

And he sought to see Jesus who He was; and could not for the press, because he was little of stature.

And he ran before, and climbed up into a sycamore tree to see Him: for Jesus was to pass that way.

And Jesus came to the place, He looked up, and saw him, and said unto him, Zacchaeus, make haste, and come down; for today I must abide at thy house." Luke 19:1-5

Rich or poor, tall or short, professional or non-professional, married or single, whole or broken, Jesus knows where you are. Even if you are under a tree, He knows where you are. Here is your proof.

"*The day following Jesus would go forth into Galilee, and findeth Philip, and saith unto him, follow me.*

Now Philip was of Bethsaida, the city of Andrew and Peter.

Philip findeth Nathaniel, and saith unto him, we have found Him, of whom Moses in the law, and the prophets, did write, Jesus of Nazareth, the son of Joseph.

And Nathaniel said unto him, can there any good thing come out of Nazareth? Philip saith unto him, come and see.

Jesus saw Nathaniel coming to Him, and saith of him, Behold an Israelite indeed, in whom is no guile!

Nathaniel saith unto Him, whence knowest thou me? Jesus answered and said unto him, Before that Philip called thee, when thou wast under the fig tree, I saw thee." John 1:43-48

Don't fret, wherever you are, Jesus knows and He sees. Whatever tree you are under, He knows. It can be the tree of loneliness, failure, abuse, debt, divorce, or grief. It doesn't really matter; He knows all about that burden you are under. Not only that, Jesus knows all about your heartache and pain, flaws, faults, and longings. He cares. You don't have to stay as you are, and you don't have to stay where you are. Jesus is there for you. He is there to bring about that change you desire in your life.

In the words of David Viscott, "You must begin to think of yourself as becoming the person you want to be." It starts in the mind. See yourself as being more than a rib. See yourself as a valuable, competent, and unique vessel of womanhood. It is important that you see yourself becoming the very woman that God created you to be. If you do not, who will? Mental elevation is a must. Do not play the blame game. Without your permission, absolutely no one can make you feel inferior or inadequate. And no one can continue to immorally use you, unless you agree.

Regardless of your past, the fact is, with Jesus your future is a clean slate. As you have already seen, Jesus proved this through the woman of Samaria. This woman had an unscrupulous past; she was unrestrained and unprincipled in her behavior. Still, Jesus forgave her past, adorned her with grace and mercy, and ushered her into a great future with Him. He will do no less for you. Jesus can and will take damaged goods and transform them into jewels. No matter how many times the devil tries to display you as being less that what God created you to be, tell him, devil, I am more than that. I am more than your lying opinion of me.

You Are!

A Woman of Perseverance

Women are perseverers. When we want something and I mean really want it, we will not allow anything to stop us. We go after that particular thing with every thing we have. We set our eyes on the goal, and off we go for the achievement. We have a spirit of determination. When the hard knocks of life take us down, we will bounce back and get up again. Block us one way and we will explore until we find another path that will lead us to our desired goal.

In Matthew chapter 15, we are introduced to a woman of perseverance. This Canaanite woman was a woman of great courage and determination. She came to Jesus to seek help for her demon possessed daughter. She was on a mission. Her plea to Jesus was, "*Have mercy on me.*" Jesus, however, did a strange and unusual thing. As a matter of fact, He did something He did not normally do when someone asked Him for help. He ignored this woman. "*He answered her not a word.*"

Not one to give up easily, she kept right on pleading her cause, so much so, that the disciples butted in. That's exactly what they did, because her appeal was to Jesus, not to them. Impatient and uncaring, they wanted to get rid of her so they asked, or rather they told Jesus to send her away. They tried to use the old brush-off approach on this woman. The fact that she was a woman of courage and determination had totally escaped the disciples. They saw a mere woman, not a woman of perseverance.

Being a woman of perseverance, naturally, she ignored the negative-minded, discouraging disciples. Falling down at Jesus' feet, she worships Him and presents her petition—again. "*Lord, help me.*" She did what she had to do. Remember, she was on a mission.

This time Jesus answered her, but the way He answered her would have caused any woman who saw herself as just a rib to give up. The Canaanite woman, however, knew something about herself. She knew within that she was more than just a rib.

Jesus' response to her was a negative one: *"It is not right to take the children's bread and cast it to dogs."* First, she was ignored, next she got the brush-off from the disciples, and then she was insulted by Jesus, the only one who could help her. But take note, she did not get an attitude, nor did she get upset. This woman of perseverance remained calm and showed humility. She was after something that was important to her. Hence, her reply, *"Truth, Lord, but even the dogs eat of the crumbs which fall from their master's table."*

I am inclined to believe that Jesus was simply testing her to see if she would stand her ground, or give up. Personally, I think this was the *how bad do you want it* test.

Jesus promptly got the answer. Boldly, she stood her ground. She refused to be deterred. She stood her ground against the silent treatment, against the discouraging disciples, and the insult. But get this, even though this woman knew she was more than just a rib, she still had a problem within herself that surfaced when she made her "eat of the crumbs" statement. Unfortunately, she was willing to settle for bits, pieces, and fragments. She had a crumb mentality. It bears repeating, mental elevation is a must.

Jesus however, looked beyond her crumb mentality and discerned her determination and courage. He then commends her with these words, *"O woman, great is thy faith, be it unto you even as thou wilt."* To put it in everyday terms, lady, you can write your own ticket.

Jesus pressed in past that crumb mentality and let her know that she could have whatever she wanted. He is still looking beyond things and stuff in our lives just so He can bless us.

Even today, Jesus wants women to get beyond the crumb mentality. He wants to help women get beyond that crumb of a job, crumb of a house, and crumb of a life. Press in past that crumb of a man—that man with the warped mentality and focus. A crumb of a man will lead to a crumb relationship, a crumb relationship will lead to a crummy marriage, and this brings about a crumble in your life.

Suddenly, your self-esteem and self-worth crumble. Your joy, hope, peace, and your dreams crumble. A crumb mentality will cause your life to become fragmented and broken. The domino effect starts. Everything collapses and falls apart. The toppling effect takes place. Every day you are hurting, sad, depressed, and frustrated. Life becomes disappointing and dissatisfying on a daily basis. Things you once enjoyed no longer satisfy you. You no longer feel alive, so you become disenchanted with life.

As a result, you find yourself settling for the wilderness while your promised land awaits you. Your dreams are crushed, and your excitement for life fades away. Rise up and be healed. Do not waste your today God has given you by living in the sorrows and regrets of yesterday. Forge on. Let go of yesterday and let go of your past. Yesterday does not matter anymore. Everyday is a brand new beginning; it is up to you, however, to make the most of your new beginning. You can either waste it, or use it to achieve something worthwhile.

The point is that God has given you another opportunity at life, so it is your move. If what you want out of life is worth having, then it is worth your determination and perseverance. Go that extra mile, or those extra ten miles if that is what it takes. Do not give up; press beyond all barriers, including the obstacles of insults, indifferences, put-downs, and taunts that you will encounter. Push past humiliation and shame inflicted on you by others. If you get knocked down, and you will, get back up and press on again.

If you receive a no in one place, proceed to the next place. If you get the brush-off over here, then find yourself going over there. For every here, there is a there. In other words, persistence pays off.

The Canaanite woman got what she wanted from Jesus because of her persistence. It will work in your life also. Jesus wants to do great and wonderful things for you, too. He delights in exercising His power, goodness, and mercy in your life.

So, if you need to fall down on your knees, fall down. And if you have to present your plea more than once, go ahead, do it. Altogether too many women allow life to pass them by because they lack courage. Refuse to quit. Refuse to give up—don't throw in the towel. Stay focused and accomplish your goal in life. Who knows, maybe someone will tell you, lady, write your own ticket, because I have seen your faith and determination.

You Have A Future

Change occurs in everyone's life. Sometimes the change is a good one and sometimes it's not. It can be a welcomed change that a person has longed for, or it can be a devastating change that was not expected. Whatever the change might be, God will provide a way to effectively deal with it. His strength, wisdom, and grace are always available to us.

Changes can come in different ways. It can occur due to the death of a spouse, divorce from a spouse, desertion by a spouse, sickness, or loss of job. Either way, women sometimes find themselves as sole breadwinners in their homes.

In First Kings chapter 17, the widow of Zarephath suffered a very devastating change in her life. Having lost her spouse through death, she found herself in a situation she had never been in before. She was now the head of her household, destitute, with a child to provide for. Not only was she the sole breadwinner, but she now had to be both mother and father to her son. She was a woman struggling to make ends meet.

Thinking she had no future, she decided to throw in the towel of defeat. In a very despondent state of mind, she went outside to gather sticks to build a fire to cook the last little food in the house for herself and her son. While the widow gathered sticks, up-stepped Elijah the prophet who asks for water and a piece of bread. Here she is, dispirited and preparing to die, and God sends someone for her to sustain. God sends to her what seems like another burden.

That which seems like one thing to us may very well turn out to be something else altogether, as it was in this case.

Explaining her situation to Elijah, she then informs him of her decision to die. *"I am gathering two sticks, that I may go in [...], eat and die."* How tragic that all she saw in her life were two sticks and death. She could not see tomorrow, nor could she see the God who held her future. A gloomy and depressing today always blinds us to our bright and hopeful tomorrows. This widow, however, had more than what she thought she had. She saw sticks and death, while God saw life and potential.

"For I know the thoughts that I think toward you, saith the Lord, thoughts of peace, and not of evil, to give you an expected end." Jeremiah 29:11

You see, God always knows what is in store for us. Even before we were born, He knew exactly the things life held for us. He knew the reality, generality, totality, as well as the finality of it all.

God, of course, had a two-fold reason for sending Elijah to Zarephath. The widow was to sustain and nourish Elijah with food, water, and shelter, while Elijah was to sustain her with life-giving words. Each had his/her own individual assignment. Man and woman need each other.

If a devastating change has occurred in your life, do not despair. You still have a future and there is a tomorrow. If all you have in your hands are two sticks, take them, fashion a cross with them, and hang it on your wall as a reminder that Jesus died and rose again to give you a future. Put hope within yourself.

"Life and death are in the power of the tongue." So tell yourself, I am coming out of this situation. You must keep hope alive, for without hope, there is no anticipation—nothing to look forward to.

The way of change we do not always know, but we know who will carry us through that change, and we know who will work all of it for our good. Usually, we are not able to see the good in the circumstance, change, or tragedy at the time it happens, but God does. It will work out, because there is victory in Jesus always. Fact is, we are not these helpless, hopeless, or powerless creatures Satan wants us to believe we are.

Learn to think like God thinks. He did not deny that there was darkness, but He spoke light. There was darkness and God simply said, *"Let there be light."* My point is, do not deny the problems, but speak answers; do not deny the sickness, but speak health and wellness; do not deny the loneliness, but speak godly companionship. You have the God-given privilege to call things that are not as though they were already a reality in your life. Oh yes, you have a future!

"Therefore I say unto you, what things soever ye desire, when ye pray, believe that ye receive them, and ye shall have them." Mark 11:24

The word *therefore* means, "for this reason." Now let's check out verses twenty-two and twenty-three.

"And Jesus answering saith unto them, Have faith in God.

For verily I say unto you, That whosoever shall say unto this mountain, Be thou removed, and be thou cast into the sea; and shall not doubt in his heart, but shall believe that those things which he saith shall come to pass; he shall have whatsoever he saith."

Jesus says to us, therefore, or for this reason—what reason? Faith. He is instilling in us that using faith, we can speak it, believe it, and have it, when it is according to His will for our lives. So, whatever you do, do not let the enemy rob you of your faith and future through circumstances, changes, or tragedies. Do not give the enemy your tomorrow, and do not prepare to die a premature death.

You have great potential as a woman. There are countless things women can accomplish in this world. As women, we are well-able and quite capable, because God, in His divine, infinite wisdom, created us to be a more than creature. Speak your tomorrows into existence and lay hold on the plan God has designed just for you. Regardless of the change that has taken place in your life, you can use that change as an opportunity to reach higher and go further in life.

What do you have in "your" hands? Go on, look. If you do not see anything else, you should see potential in those hands; potential to make a difference in your home, as well as in society.

One woman in the Bible by the name of Miriam only had a timbrel in her hand, but she used it.

"And Miriam the prophetess, the sister of Aaron, took a timbrel in her hand; and all the women went out after her with timbrels and with dances." Exodus 15:20

Only a timbrel in her hand, yet she led *all* the women. Miriam had zeal and inspiration, leadership skills, and she had a ministering spirit. She had flaws, but her abilities were greater than her flaws. She used what was in her hand to enhance the lives of those around her.

Even as a young girl, Miriam knew she was destined to be more than just a rib. Exodus Chapter two verses one through eight reveals this truth. Her intellect and courage are highlighted in verses four and seven.

"And his sister stood afar off, to wit what would be done to him. (Verse 4)

"Then said his sister to Pharoah's daughter, Shall I go up and call to thee a nurse of the Hebrew women, that she may nurse the child for thee?" (Verse 7)

Everything Miriam had was there in her from childhood. Her inner strength, fearlessness, and her intelligence were evident. Do not ever say that you don't have anything because you do. It's just a matter of finding out what it is that you do have. I don't have anything in my hand but a writing pen, but I am using it.

God can and will take your little bit and turn it into much. He is a God of addition and multiplication.

Now, look again. What do you see in your hands this time? Go for it. God wants us to be women of courage and faith.

Remember, while the widow of Zarephath was trying to give up and die, her deliverance was on the way. God had already put her tomorrow into action. Your tomorrow has been activated, too. Hold on!

Just Do It

Many women suffer from what I call the *less than syndrome*. The less than syndrome is when you have a problem believing that God created you to be worthwhile, valuable, capable, whole, intelligent, and complete. A woman suffering from the less than syndrome is incapable of accepting her God-given image and divine assessment. She finds it hard to believe that she is gifted, talented, and intelligent. Feelings of incompetence, insecurity, and inadequacy plague her on a daily basis. Having an unhealthy assessment of herself, she is always filled with negativity.

Unfortunately, she allows Satan or others to minimize her divine worth as a woman. Allow me to illustrate my point.

Luke 7:36-39

"And one of the Pharisees desired Jesus that He would eat with him. And He went up into the Pharisee's house, and sat down to meat.

And, behold, a woman in the city, which was a sinner, when she knew that Jesus sat at meat in the Pharisee's house, brought an alabaster box of ointment.

And stood at His feet behind Him weeping, and began to wash His feet with tears, and did wipe them with the hairs of her head, and kissed His feet, and anointed them with the ointment.

Now when the Pharisee which had bidden Him saw it, he spoke within himself, saying, This man, if He were a prophet, would have known who and what manner of woman this is that touched Him: for she is a sinner."

First of all, this Pharisee was a judgmental, opinionated, self-righteous, finger-pointing man. In his self-righteous assessment, this woman was small, insignificant, and degrading. He made her feel as if she was not worthy of desiring a better life for herself. His condescending attitude implied that she was unworthy of higher expectations in life.

This writer is happy to know that the word *lied* is included in the word implied for women everywhere. How sad it is when a woman allows condescending attitudes and biased opinions of others to keep her trapped in the less than syndrome. She let things, mess-ups, and people define who and what she is in life. Instead of allowing God's Word to define, assess, and identify her, she falls victim to finite, imperfect opinions given by finite, imperfect people.

Unfortunately, the woman presented in Luke Chapter Seven allowed herself to become something God never intended her to become. She allowed herself to be used by men to satisfy their sexual lust. Because of an inappropriate view she had of herself, her reputation became tarnished, and she was labeled by society as "that kind of woman." Society will brand any woman who suffers from the less than syndrome. The same people who use her, will in turn, brand her.

Therefore, she suffers the loss of her good name, self-respect, clean reputation, and morals, simply because she saw herself as just a rib. The less than syndrome will diminish a woman's true worth. It reduces a woman mentally, emotionally, physically, and spiritually. As long as a woman suffers from this syndrome, she will never reach her God-given potential.

Ladies, this is a wake-up call. Before you can get up and go up, you first must wake-up. Fortunately, this society-branded woman came to Jesus to get delivered from her less than syndrome. That was wise of her, because deliverance is the only way.

While some women have this problem, others do not. There are women who know that they are more than and not less than.

In Judges Chapter Four, Deborah was such a woman. She did not have a less than mentality. Deborah held and functioned in several divine seats and positions. She was a judge, prophetess, ruler, motivator, warrior, poetess, and wife.

Moving busily and effectively from place to place in her divinely given seats and positions, Deborah impacted the lives of those around her. This is one woman who did not eat the bread of idleness. God raised her up to hold high profiled positions. Her leadership skills in political, military, civil, and religious spheres were admirable, to say the least. In addition, this successful, influential, and powerful woman also sat in the seat of wifehood. Evidently, she must have occupied this seat well, using wisdom and giving respect and honor to her husband, Lapidoth. Nowhere do we read that he complained or was neglected in any way.

This more than woman was aggressive, determined, and strong-willed with the spirit of humility. Humility will put you over every time.

As you can see, Deborah was a woman of many abilities and skills; she was also very intelligent, and her intelligence was enhanced by her out-going and illuminative personality. Not only that, Deborah was a woman who knew who she was, what she was, and what she was capable of accomplishing. She was divinely empowered to do all these things successfully, and she recognized this fact (See Judges 5). If God puts you there, you can effectively deal with the positions, the people, and the pressure. It can be done!

If you are a woman suffering from the less than syndrome, I recommend you go to the Bible, the greatest book ever written, and discover exactly who and what you are and all the things you are capable of accomplishing.

Delve into the Word of God and see for yourself who you are in Christ. Let me assure you that God in His written Word defines, assesses, and identifies what a woman is, should be, and can be in life.

Women, you have achieving power, overcoming power, and conquering power. If life knocks you down, get back up and brush yourself off in the love and forgiveness of

Jesus. He does not have a problem reaching down when you need picking up. There is lifting available to you from Jesus.

By far, there are too many hurting, miserable women in this world; not because of some man, not because of some job, not because of financial lack, and not even because you want to or have to be miserable. You are this way because, unwittingly, you have mentally allowed yourself to become less than. In all actuality, you are really unhappy with yourself, and when a woman is unhappy with herself, she becomes dissatisfied with most things around her.

Remedy the situation. Rise above the less than syndrome to the more than power of God, and watch yourself become all that your Creator made you to be. You will become more empowered than you ever imaged yourself capable.

If society has branded you, you do not have to stay branded; if the church has labeled you because of divorce or other factors, you do not have to wear the label; and if you have fallen, you do not have to stay down. Arise! Your seat is empty and waiting for you to occupy it, and your divine mantle is waiting to wrap itself around your shoulders.

Do not forget this—*"Male and female created He them. And God blessed them, and God said unto them, be fruitful, multiply, replenish, subdue, and have dominion."* T-h-e-m. In other words, the focus here is not on man alone. God created and blessed *them*, and said unto *them*. As you can see, the focus is on both man and woman.

Look at the order in which God put these commands.

First, multiply. God told both man and woman to produce and increase in the things of life.

Second, be fruitful. Again, the command is to both male and female. Both were to be productive and prolific, not barren or idle. This was a command for them to be bountiful, fertile, plenteous, and rich in every arena of life.

Third, replenish. Both man and woman were to restock or reproduce what was lacking. Together they were to fill again or fill anew that which had been used.

Fourth, subdue. Again, both man and woman were to unite to defeat anything that threatened their togetherness and oneness. As a team, they were to conquer, overcome, and overpower anything that posed a threat to their unity.

Last, have dominion. Male and female were to rule together. Each one had an arena to control and influence, and each one could occupy a commanding position. Any way you look, it comes up t-h-e-m, male and female, man and woman.

A good example of "t-h-e-m" is Priscilla and Aquila (See Acts 18:2, 18, 26; Romans 16:3; First Corinthians 16:19; Second Timothy 4:19). This husband and wife were truly a team. Truth, when women do these five things, we are not living contrary to God's Word. Quite the opposite, as a matter of fact. When woman multiplies, is fruitful, is productive, replenishes, subdues, and has dominion, she is only complying and submitting to God's Word.

Throughout the Bible, you will find where God placed different women in positions that called for them to do all these things.

Woman is by no means less than man; nor is she inferior or superior to him. God gave both male and female great inner potential. A woman's mind, intelligence, gifts, talents, and abilities are not beneath the man's. When woman is referred to as the weaker vessel, it simply means she does not have the brute, physical strength that a man has. Her physical body is not as strong as the man's body. A woman is delicate, soft, and easily damaged when handled roughly. And while she is efficient in physical bodily strength, she is not necessarily deficient in moral strength or emotional endurance. Spiritually, women are more enduring and more steadfast than men (See Jeremiah 9:1-8; 12:20; Luke 24:10-11; Mark 16: 9-11).

Both sexes can have weak minds, and both sexes have weak flesh. Men, as well as women, are prone to make unwise choices and decisions. So ladies, rid yourselves of that less than syndrome; and whatever you have been called by God to do, do it.

That is exactly what Deborah did. If she was criticized, and I am sure she was, she kept going because she had a job to do. Besides, you cannot allow petty criticism from others to stop you from achieving and accomplishing.

If you have been placed in a seat of honor, serve well while in that seat; and if you have been given a position, work the position. The authority you have been given was given to you to use. You, however, need to use that authority with humility and respectability. Do not throw your weight around just because you can. Let somebody else know something besides you. That is called being secure in who you are and what you have been anointed and gifted to do.

Take Huldah, for example. She had the authority and ministry of a prophetess and she walked in that authority. Still, she exercised her authority with dignity and humility. Huldah allowed nothing to intimidate her in her God-ordained position. When the lost book of the law was discovered, it was Huldah that King Josiah called upon. After reading the contents, Huldah prophesied that Judah would experience national ruin because of their disobedience and waywardness (See Second Kings 22:14-20). King Josiah consulted Huldah about the matter because she occupied that particular God-assigned position of prophetess. As you can see, God is not a biased, gender-oriented God. Often He will anoint and appoint a woman in a so-called man's position and when He does, He expects that woman to occupy the seat without intimidation from anyone. It is His call as well as His choice, as you will see after reading Huldah's prophesy.

"And she said unto them, Thus saith the Lord God of Israel, Tell the man that sent you to me,

Thus saith the Lord, Behold I will bring evil upon this place, and upon the inhabitance thereof, even all the words of the book which the King of Judah hath read:

Because they have forsaken me, and have burned incense unto other gods, that they might provoke me to anger with all the works of their hands; therefore my wrath shall be kindled against this place, and shall not be quenched" (Second Kings 22:15-17).

Not a welcomed message, but she fearlessly operated within her assigned authority and did what she had to do.

Likewise, many of you will find yourselves in seats of authority usually occupied by men, and you will have to make decisions that will not be easy. Do not be afraid; seek God's divine wisdom and make the decisions you need to make. Make them honorably and humbly, but make them fearlessly.

Proverbs 3:5-6 tells us this: *"Trust in the Lord with all thine heart; and lean not unto thine own understanding.*

In all thy ways acknowledge Him, and He shall direct thy paths."

This is well-worth mentioning. Before some women were even conceived in their mother's womb, God had ordained that they should and would hold certain so-called men only positions. Therefore, as women, we will be given opportunities in every arena of life to function in our God-ordained seats and positions of authority. We will be called on as mothers, wives, teachers, principals, supervisors, consultants, judges, mayors, presidents, and CEOs to lead, make decisions, and to take charge.

For instance, we will have to say no sometimes when others think we should have said yes; decline certain things instead of accepting those things; and refusing an offer instead of going along with the crowd. We will be called on to hire, fire, promote, and demote. So, if you are sitting in the seat, you will have to occupy it, or relinquish it.

Accept the fact that even when you function in your seat in a proper and effective manner, you will encounter opposition. Any position of authority will have opposition from combative forces. These combative forces strike because of jealousy, hatred, ignorance, fear, or prejudices. Nonetheless, you must occupy your seat and position of authority with courage. Remember, any seat of authority also brings about many challenges. Face every challenge in the strength and wisdom of God. You can, because all God-given assignments come with His enablement.

Emulate Deborah and Huldah, maintain the right attitude, and do whatever it is you need to do. Let service, honor, and righteousness be your garments; and when you open your mouth, open it with wisdom and kindness. Know this, you can be firm and still be kind. Be strong, yes, but also be wise. Man and woman should not compete with each other. Like Priscilla and Aquila, man and woman are to complement each other.

Neither should feel intimidated in the position God has placed him or her. Deborah boldly occupied every office and position she held. So can you—just do it.

Classy and Courageous

God gave woman a distinction of her own, and this distinction cannot be compared to anything else. God gave woman the ability and intelligence to make a worthwhile and enduring difference in this world. In His infinite wisdom, God provided woman with an inner strength and a divine mark of special favor unlike any other creature. Woman was given a place of honor and eminence, as well as a station of elevation. Because woman is a creature of noteworthy femininity, courage, and strength, womanhood is to be celebrated, not desecrated.

Esther is a good example of a woman with divine distinction. She was well-bred, elegant, and refined. She was both classy and courageous (Read Esther 2:7-17). Esther was also a woman of ingenuity. She possessed an aptitude of cleverness, resourcefulness, and imagination. She was innocent, but not naïve; straightforward, but not crass; and she was cunning, but she was not a schemer. There was an efficiency about this classy and courageous woman.

Esther had knack. There was a readiness within her that propelled her to do whatever needed to be done, even at the possible cost of her own life.

Esther means star, and indeed a star she was. She was a star of hope to her people and a star of joy to king Ahasuerus. She was not just outer beauty alone, but she possessed inner beauty as well. Her name fitted her like a person's skin fits her body. It was an adequate name given to an adequate woman.

Being a woman of clear judgment, self-control, fasting, and prayer, Esther was a woman in "the know." She knew how to confront her problems skillfully and prayerfully. She knew that outer beauty fades, while inner beauty shines on. And she knew it took more than a beautiful face and sexy body to confront problems triumphantly. Esther was a rare individual for sure. Seemingly, she had it all. She had charm, courage, beauty, and dignity, in addition to strength and sensuality. She was aggressive, yet she maintained her elegance and refinement.

When beauty cannot make a difference, Esther proved for all women that prayer can and will. She demonstrated that a woman cannot and must not depend on her good looks and great figure to get her through life. Being the woman of determination that she was, she dared to risk death for her people's future.

"*If I perish, I perish,*" was her unique and bold battle cry. However, before she confronted the crisis, she prepared herself for the crisis because she knew that prayer and fasting turns a defeated woman into a determined, victorious force. As the king's wife, Esther had a position of power and eminence, and she skillfully used that position of power and eminence for the good and well-being of others.

Esther knew and proved that she was more than just a rib. In the hour of turmoil, she stood strong, sought divine guidance, and obtained an astonishing deliverance for her nation.

Married to the same man that was once married to Vashti, Esther, however, was not just a second wife. Still, she and Vashti were alike in many ways. Both were beautiful, intelligent women; both carried themselves with dignity and respect; and both knew they were women of distinction. However, there was one major difference between the two women—Esther was godly and prayerful, whereas Vashti was more laxed and made her own rules. Esther knew the power of influence a woman possesses and used it. She did her homework.

Carefully, she observed king Ahasuerus and gained valuable knowledge about his nature, personality, and character. By carefully observing and studying Ahasuerus, she got to know the man inside the physique. Esther entered into this marriage, not with just her heart, but also with her head. She made knowing her man her top priority, thereby gaining his backing and support during her crisis. Not only was she intelligent, but she was also wise.

Pardon my language, ladies, but there is more to you than your "Josephine," and there is more to a man, or there should be, than his "Johnson."

Even though Ahasuerus fell for Esther because of her beauty and fine body, Esther knew that there was more to her than just those things.

If a man does not know, you must know; and if he cannot see beyond the other things, you must be sure about the inner things. If you are not sure about your inner qualities, that man will depict you as a rib only, and unfortunately, you will buy into that lie, also.

Now for the big question: *Is God really looking for women with a more than conviction?* You better believe He is. He is a more than God, and He wants some courageous, determined women with a godly aggressiveness.

In Matthew chapter eleven and verse twelve, we read these words—*"The kingdom of heaven suffereth violence, and the violent take it by force."*

The violent, or the aggressive ones, take it by force-- the force of prayer, fasting, boldness, determination, perseverance, and illumination.

There must be illumination. Before you can effectively accomplish anything great, you need to be informed. Your mission or ministry must be clear in your mind and spirit. There are too many women making moves without first clarifying their goal. To achieve, we must be enlightened and informed.

Jeremiah chapter nine and verse seventeen clearly makes us aware that there is a need in the kingdom for cunning, persistent women with a more than conviction and attitude. So, allow no one to tell you that you do not have a ministry or divine purpose in life. You do, but clarity first, please.

Also, realize and remember that life is not all smiles. It is a mixture of both sweet and sour experiences and we must deal with both, because sooner or later, reality will hit home in your life.

Expecting everything in life to be sweet and wonderful is not facing reality. Reality is the real stuff or the real issues and battles, and when we come face to face with the real thing, we must deal with it as Esther did in her crisis.

As women, without really meaning to, we have a tendency to look at life through rose-tinted glasses. Still, reality always sets in. Trials start, harsh circumstances come, heartbreak arrives, and choices stare us in the face. Stop or continue, quit or persevere, forge on or turn back, give up, give in, get out, or give it another try? The enemy will tell you to quit, reality says that decisions are just a part of life, but faith and your more than conviction about God and yourself say hold fast, for with much affliction you attain the goal.

You see, God allows reality to set in because He wants us to realize that life is not a fairy tale. I am sure you know the story of Cinderella. On the night of the grand ball, Cinderella is not allowed to attend. Her evil stepmother and two cruel, selfish stepsisters prevent her from attending the ball. Naturally, Cinderella's heart is broken and she starts to cry. But wait! All is not lost. Her "fairy" godmother appears, waives a "magic wand," says a few "magic words," and transforms Cinderella into a beautiful princess.

Cinderella is then whisked off to the ball in her "magic pumpkin coach," and there she meets her prince charming. The story ends with Cinderella and prince charming getting married and living happily ever after.

It stands repeating, real life is not a fairy tale. We cannot afford to go through life with a fairy tale mentality. Life deals with reality—severe trials, harsh circumstances, troubles, and death, with its grief and sorrow. It deals with heartbreaks, broken covenants, vows, as well as crushed dreams. In real life there are no fairy godmothers, magic wands, or magic words. However, there is God, and with Him we can face reality no matter how grim it might be for us. No magic words and no magic wand to give that so-called magic touch; but the Word of God along with the power of God are available to us to work in our lives, and these two resources are more than enough.

In Isaiah chapter thirty-two and verses nine through eleven, we find this command and warning—*"Rise up ye women that are at ease; hear my voice, ye careless daughters; give ear unto my speech.*

Many days and years shall ye be troubled, ye careless women; for the vintage shall fail, the gathering shall not come.

Tremble, ye women that are at ease; be troubled, ye careless ones, strip you, and make you bare, and gird sackcloth upon your loins."

Without doubt, reality will hit home, and God will be looking for some courageous and aggressive Esthers. Women that will rise up, become concerned and take the necessary steps required to do something about the conditions around their environment. Do you have an Esther attitude? Do you have a more than conviction like Esther? If the answer is yes, then God wants to use you. He is looking for women with an attitude of—I am going, and if I perish, I perish. God, in other words, is looking for that woman who is willing to take a risk and a stand; one that will not shrink back because of implied consequences. Besides, who knows whether or not you have come into your place of position for such a time as this?

One thing for sure, wherever you are today, there is a divine reason for being there. That job you are on where certain people are giving you a hard time, could it be that you are there to be divinely used to bring deliverance to them? Could it be that God is using you to be a light in all that darkness? That company you are working for, it's possible that it's headed for bankruptcy, and God has you there to give you a divine idea that can be implemented to keep that company productive.

Our steps are divinely orchestrated and our seasons are in His hand. So wherever you are could be your assignment for this season of your life.

Understand this, divine aggressiveness is a good thing to possess. It was because of Esther's God-given aggressiveness that the Jewish nation was saved from genocide. The aggressiveness and courage of a woman kept them alive. She took their destiny out of the enemy's hand by force, and that force was the power of prayer along with brave action.

Esther got aggressive and did what she had to do. She dared to appear before the king without being summoned, she dared to present her petition, and she dared to invite her enemy to dinner.

Well-bred, elegant, and refined, but when reality hit home, she got aggressive. The woman got feisty. She did not kick against the prick, meaning she did not go against authority that was in place. Esther, however, went against the grain and won. She refused to accept the death warrant concept that was being forced on her.

Like Esther, we must be willing to do the same, because when there is a great calling on your life, you can look for great trials. If God has endowed you with great influence, look for great persecution. It comes with the territory. Being woman does not exempt you from having to deal with harsh realities. Life on earth was not meant to be smooth sailing all the time. There will always be problems, unwelcome circumstances, heartbreaking ordeals, as well as challenges and changes.

There are always choices to make—the wilderness or the promised land, the garlic or the grapes, failure or success, defeat or deliverance, the enemy or the Enabler. Sad to say, but some would rather choose the enemy instead of the Enabler.

Also, when reality hits home, be careful how you "see" it. You can either see through the eyes of fear, or through the eyes of faith; through the eyes of a quitter, or through the eyes of an overcomer; through the eyes of a victim, or through the eyes of a victor. Be careful how you look at life.

In Numbers chapter thirteen, the children of Israel saw through the wrong eyes. In verse thirty-one, they said in essence, we are not, for they—the giants—are; and in verse thirty-three, they said, we saw, so we were. They saw the giants, and in their wrong estimation or conclusion of who they were, they saw themselves as grasshoppers. They were God's chosen people, yet they concluded they were grasshoppers. Reality will diminish and swallow you up when you see through the wrong eyes.

When reality hits home, God wants us to see Him as Jesus saw Him. Jesus constantly bragged on His Daddy. My Father can; My Father will; My Father sees; My Father knows. He hears Me always, and He is with Me all the time. My Father this and My Father that—that is exactly the way God wants to be. He has not ceased being active on our behalf. As a matter of fact, His power and love still embrace us, and He yet achieves our good when we persist in seeking His heart.

God offers His help to us in every kind of trouble. He sends challenges our way to prove us, not to intimidate us. It is the enemy who takes these challenges and then uses them to threaten, intimidate, and diminish us. But every time reality hits home, our divine Daddy accesses the circumstance. He sees the situation not as a problem, but as an opportunity for us to trust Him and allow Him to bring glory to His name. He sees the potential in the situation for our life—potential to build character because He knows that everyone of us has an Achilles' heel.

Therefore, we need to stay in the press, continue in faith, stay aggressive and feisty, and keep believing. Regardless of what we see when reality hits home, God wants us to see the full potential of His power at work in our circumstance.

In any case, when your reality hits home, do not panic. God will test it, bless it, and then rest it for you, after it has accomplished its purpose in your life. He will get you through any situation. I know this for a fact.

How we see—through the eyes of faith; who we see—God at work in our situation; and what we see—victory, always, are all important to our outcome. We can see giants or we can see God; we can see potential or we can see nothing but the problem; we can see obstacles or we can see opportunities. If we see ourselves as less than what God sees (and He sees overcomers and "more than" conquerors), Satan will then use how we see ourselves to defeat us.

Esther knew who and what she was in life because of God, her Enabler. So must we. She knew that she had been created by a *more than* God that was backing her with His *more than* power to help her be that *more than* woman in every reality life threw at her.

A fitting tribute to Esther is: a more than woman who relied on prayer and divine power, instead of her beauty. This is an appropriate tribute for any woman who knows who and what she was created to be in life. My personal motto is—just let me be woman.

Shameful Past – Shining Future

Rahab is another woman who suffered from the less than syndrome. Rahab was a harlot. Simply put, she was a prostitute, according to Joshua 2:1-6. She willingly yielded her body for money so that men could satisfy their lust. Being another one of society's so-called outcasts, the men used her, and the prim and proper respectable women in the community shunned her. Let's put it another way, the good, up-standing women looked down on her, while the prominent men slept with her. They had to be prominent men; men of financial means, because "high class" prostitutes do not come cheap. Rahab did not come cheap. This is inferred by scriptural stated location and description of her house.

Rahab, nevertheless, was a woman to be reckoned with. People in the city had to deal with her from the king on down. Even though she had a flawed character, evident in the way she was openly referred to as Rahab, the harlot, there was also a kindness in her heart. She had an inner softness, despite her immoral lifestyle.

Rahab was a prostitute with great potential, and it was no accident, co-incidence, or fluke that the spies went to her house. A prostitute is devious. They deal with people in a roundabout and indirect way. They are cunning, foxy, and shrewd. Out of all the houses in the city, God led the spies to this woman's house.

Remember what I said earlier about God not only knows who you are, but He also knows exactly where you are? Purposely, the spies were led there by God because they needed someone who knew the ins-and-outs of the city. They needed someone who was shrewd and cunning enough to get them in and out without being detected. They needed someone who was devious and willing to take a risk—they needed Rahab.

There is a truth that needs to be comprehended here, and that truth is, only God can see beyond the flawed character of a person to the kind heart in that person. He can and often does take a character trait that an individual is using for evil purposes and uses it for a good purpose. Somehow, He can take that which is being used in a bad way and utilize it to bring good to others. That is exactly what God did with Rahab. He utilized her skills to protect the spies and help them escape safely. Rahab, the harlot, had great potential for good and God brought that potential to the surface.

We do well when we remember that there is always at least one commendable trait in the supposedly worst kind of woman. Even when she has been hardened by life's sorrows, pains, disappointments, and devastations, there is something else to be discovered. Even when she has been kicked in the teeth over and over and finds herself turning coarser and coarser, there is something else there. There is an inner softness. You may have to probe deeply to find it, but it is there; tucked down deep within her inner-self just waiting to surface and make itself known to somebody. Despite the crude, rough, rude, and unrefined conduct, there is an inner softness.

Of course, it takes someone wise and special to find it, and that someone is God. While others point the finger of criticism and rebuke, God offers grace and mercy. His mercies are new every morning. This is why new beginnings are at our disposal everyday. God can give you a shining future even if you have a shameful past. Indeed, your past does not have to be your future. God knows what to do with your past, and how to give you a future. Everyone has fallen short of God's ideals and sinned.

John 8:3-11

"And the scribes and Pharisees brought unto Jesus a woman taken in adultery; and when they had set her in the midst,

They said unto Him, Master, this woman was taken in adultery, in the very act.

Now Moses in the law commanded us, that such should be stoned: but what sayest thou?

This they said, tempting Him, that they might have to accuse Him, but Jesus stooped down, and with His finger wrote on the ground, as though He heard them not.

So when they continued asking Him, He lifted up Himself, and said unto them, He that is without sin among you, let him first cast a stone at her.

And again He stooped down, and wrote on the ground.

And they which heard it, being convicted by their own conscience, went out one by one, beginning at the eldest, even unto the last: and Jesus was left alone, and the woman standing in the midst.

When Jesus had lifted up himself, and saw no one but the woman, He said unto her, Woman, where are those thine accusers? hath no man condemned thee?

She said, No man, Lord. And Jesus said unto her, Neither do I condemn thee: go, and sin no more."

"Go and sin no more." Here we see Jesus exhibiting love and compassion, yet giving this firm command. Being who and what He is, Jesus gave this woman an opportunity for a shining future, because His grace was greater than her disgrace. He saw her inner softness.

She saw, too. Somehow she knew she was in the company of someone who would not point the finger of accusation. She sensed something about Jesus even before he spoke those words to her.

Notice in verse three it says—"they <u>set</u> her in the midst." Set, meaning, they—the scribes and Pharisees, had placed or put her there. However, in verse nine it says, "[…] and the woman <u>standing</u> in the midst […]." Suddenly, she was no longer in the position they had put her in, but she had stood up. She was standing erect; something about Jesus reached this woman's inner-self.

She walked in with her head down, but before it was over, the situation had been remedied. She was now standing with a sense of worthiness down on the inside. It finally dawned on her that she was more than what the scribes and Pharisees positioned her to be in life. Caught in the act, but—I am more than that; guilty as charged, but—I am more than that. Somehow she knew.

So must you. You must know for yourself, because if you do not, others will try to tell you what you are in life. If you do not define yourself, people will "set you in the midst," and proceed to define you.

Being in the presence of Jesus is an awesome place to be for anyone. It was in the presence of Jesus that realization set in for this woman. She realized that one foolish mistake did not have to ruin her life. Jesus always brings out the best in you. He will bring to light those things that are hidden even to yourself. Even in the supposedly worst kind of woman, there is something good in her to be discovered, and Jesus is the One to find that good.

If you have a shameful past, it's alright to hold your head up. God says it's alright for you to hold up your head. God says to lift up your head; not in arrogant pride, but in godly expectation and anticipation. Now the word *lift* means, "to raise or direct upward; to raise in rank, condition, and estimation." Remember these three words—rank, condition, and estimation.

In Psalms 24:7-8, we read these words. *"Lift up your heads, O ye gates; and be ye lift up, ye everlasting doors; and the King of glory shall come in. Who is this King of glory? The Lord strong and mighty, the Lord mighty in battle."*

Here we have an "if you will, then I will" situation. When you lift up your head, you will be lifted up. Your spirit will be elevated to a new level and that old downward, degrading, and self-loathing feeling will vanish. God will deposit divine esteem and joy within you. He will help you to see that you are valuable and important to Him, if not to anybody else.

Remember the woman in Luke chapter seven? This woman had been labeled a street woman because of her less than mentality and lifestyle. Since she had an unhealthy, negative image of herself, she in turn lived as she saw herself.

Norman Vincent Peale gave timeless and valuable advice when he said, "Be sure to imagine right, for we tend to become as we see ourselves." How true this statement, as we can see from this woman's life. She had been labeled, and unfortunately, she lived out the label. Only God knows exactly how long she had worn this negative label. He also knows how the labeling got started. It is possible that she became intimately involved with a man whom she loved and he in turn trashed her reputation.

Do not get me wrong, I am not condoning her conduct, but one mistake does not make a woman a harlot. Sadly, the label stuck and because she believed the label, she kept on wallowing. Still, there was something within that kept propelling her to get up and change paths. Scripture states, "*She stood at Jesus' feet behind Him weeping, and began to wash His feet with her tears […].*"

She stood behind Jesus. The less than mentality is still kicking in, still holding her prisoner, but not for long. Who knows how many tears she had shed before she caved in and accepted this people-given label. Weeping and washing Jesus' feet with tears running down her face, she was dealing with her pain and looking for a way of escape out of that lifestyle. Jesus knew exactly what she wanted and needed from Him—"*Wherefore I say unto thee, Her sins, which are many, are forgiven; for she loved much […].*" He boldly states, her sins are many, indicating that she had fallen into a habit of this kind of lifestyle.

How tragic that this woman allowed people to define who and what she was. Jesus did not deny her lifestyle for He admitted her sins were many, but He did not label her either. Jesus got beyond the exterior to the interior and gave an explanation for her actions. Notice, He gave an explanation, not an excuse, and that explanation was, "For she loved much." This misguided woman had a tender and giving heart. It is of little wonder that men found her to be an easy mark for their sexual pleasures. Still, I am convinced she lost sleep many nights trying to figure out a way to regain her God-given worth and value that she had lost.

Eventually, her desire for a different lifestyle led her to Jesus. When she found out that Jesus was in the Pharisee's house, she entered without waiting for an invitation. Good thing she did, because she never would have received one from this man. He saw her as defiled, corrupt, and insignificant. Jesus, on the other hand, saw her as one reaching out for something better in life, and He gave it to her.

Jesus wants to do the same for you. He longs to lift up your head so that He can come in and give you a relationship with Him. So lift up your head, ye gates and doors. A door is any means of approach or access, and a gate is an opening or entrance. Hence, the three words I wanted you to remember.

First, condition. It means, "to put in a proper state."

Second, rank. This is a position or standing in the social arena. "To take up or occupy a place."

Third, estimation. "The forming of an opinion."

The woman in John, chapter eight, was confronted with all three elements. Her condition was sinful, so she needed to be re-established properly. Her rank on the social scale was low because she had been caught in the act of adultery, so she was forced by the scribes and Pharisees to occupy a place of embarrassment temporarily. Also, they had formed an inaccurate and low opinion of her.

Nevertheless, it is never over until Jesus says it is over. When Jesus finished talking to this woman, He had given her a way out of her previous condition, "Go and sin no more." Jesus takes care of every detail, so He did not stop there. He elevated her rank on the social scale, also. Not one of her accusers was sinless; not one of them had the right to point an accusing finger; and not one of them could throw a stone at her guiltless. They were no different, nor were they any better than she. They were all sinners.

Very expertly, Jesus took care of the last detail, which was the estimation detail. He let her know that people's opinions do not count for much when compared to His. His estimation of her was that she was worthy of a second chance. Jesus, therefore, said unto her, "I refuse to condemn you." Amazing, isn't it? The only one that could condemn her, did not condemn her. She was no longer where they had put her; Jesus left her standing. He never leaves you where He finds you. You are always left better after being in His presence.

Unfortunately, there are far too many things in life that can cause us to walk around with hung down heads. Someone may have spread malicious gossip about you, or told an embarrassing lie on you. It could be that your marriage has ended, or you could be dealing with an unfaithful spouse, or you may have lost your job. Some of you are hurting, some of you are feeling degraded, and others are lonely and feeling suicidal.

Enough is enough. God longs to lift and elevate your spirit. He wants to give you that second chance. He desires to reach down, pick you up, and leave you standing. Yes, weapons are being formed against you all the time, but they will not prosper in your life. God can and will change your condition. He will change your condition on the social scale, and He will change your negative opinion about yourself. The king of glory wants to be in your life. He wants to get in your situation, your heartbreak, and your hurt. When God gets in your situation, people have to get out of it.

It is essential that you understand that God is not intimidated or embarrassed by your circumstances. There is absolutely nothing about your life that can shock Him. He already knows everything about you. He knows all about the malicious gossip that is going around about you. He knows about the break-up of your marriage and He knows that you are contemplating suicide. Even though God is not shocked,

He is concerned; and though He will not condemn you, He will certainly deliver you, if you let Him.

You have an invitation to come boldly to the throne of grace and the table of mercy. The invitation is a standing one. Never mind those self-righteous, holier-than-thou upstanding church folk who are ready to point the finger of criticism and accusation. In any case, you have the right to come because Jesus gave it to you.

Romans 5:8, clearly states—*"But God commendeth His love toward us, in that, while we were yet sinners, Christ died for us."* In other words, it is already taken care of for you. You do not have to stay where you are, and no one has the right to forcibly bring you to Jesus. You have the right to come on your own.

Jesus came to give you abundant life and this includes a better condition, another rank, and a greater estimation of life with Him.

Rahab got her second chance in life. Eventually, her eyes opened, she saw herself as she was, and then she saw herself as she was meant to be. She finally realized that she had a purpose and a destiny, and it was not to live as a prostitute or operate a house of ill-repute. At last, she knew that she was a woman to be held in high esteem. She became a godly woman, married Salmon (one of the spies she protected), and gave birth to Boaz, who in turn fathered Obed. Obed fathered Jesse, and of course, Jesse fathered David, the king.

It was through this royal line of genealogy that Jesus came into the world. Rahab, the harlot, was a part of the family tree of Jesus. She went from being a rib to be an ancestress of Christ. In the Old Testament, she is a prostitute, and in the New Testament, she is listed as a heroine of faith.

Your shameful past does not have to follow you around, either. If you do not like being the way you are, again I say to you, you have the right—a God-given right—to do something about it. The grace of God is no respecter of persons. It is available to everyone and anyone. When you boldly come to the throne of God, without caring what people think about you, Jesus will take the shameful past and put it into the sea of divine forgetfulness, just so you can walk away with a shining future before you.

"*I am the light of the world: he*[she] *that followeth me shall not walk in darkness, but shall have the light of life,*" states John 8:12. Why live in shame when you can have Jesus, the light of life? Can anyone condemn you because of your past and be counted guiltless? No! Absolutely not, because we all have sinned and fallen short. Here is your scriptural proof, found in Philippians 3:13-14.

"*I count not myself to have apprehended: but this one thing I do, forgetting those things which are behind, and reaching forth unto those things which are before.*

I press toward the mark for the prize of the high calling of God in Christ Jesus."

Refuse to wear other people's labels. If you want to wear a label, wear this one—made in the image of God. Now go ahead, leave your past behind, walk away in the power of God, and go for your shining future.

Presenting the Verdict

The harvest is past, the summer is ended, and we are not saved.

For the hurt of the daughter of my people am I hurt; I am black; astonishment hath taken hold on me.

Is there no balm in Gilead; is there no physician there? Why then is not the health of the daughters of my people recovered?

Jeremiah 8:20-22

Exposing the Truth

For I know the thoughts that I think toward you, saith the Lord, thoughts of peace, and not of evil, to give you an expected end.

Then shall ye call upon me, and ye shall go and pray unto me, and I will hearken unto you.

And ye shall seek me, and find me, when ye shall search for me with all of your heart.

And I will be found of you, saith the Lord: and I will turn away your captivity.

Jeremiah 29:11-14b

Divine Persistence For A Divine Destiny

Many of you are feeling desperate, frustrated, depressed, and defeated. You are in a hard and difficult place and you feel like you are barely surviving. Then, there are those who are on the verge of a mental and emotional collapse. Everything in you is shutting down and you feel yourself going under. Don't! Do not go under and do not shut down, God has a plan for your life. He never intended for you to barely survive. He has so much more in mind for you.

Indeed, God has a plan, but before His plan for your life starts to emerge, you need to come out from under some things. Some of you have buried the real you under the layers of self-pity and self-protection. You have been badly hurt, so you are trying to keep yourself from ever being hurt again. You have walled yourself up, hoping that nothing will ever penetrate that wall. You do not want anything to touch your emotions or your heart.

Have courage. You are not alone in your dilemma. Unfortunately, there are others in the same predicament as you, only they have themselves buried under layers of self-condemnation. They are always down on themselves, finding fault with everything they do even when they do it well. They do not appreciate their worth. And then others are under layers of envy and jealousy, slowly dying on the inside. They are this way because they feel like they do not measure up; therefore, they will not allow themselves to be happy about the success of others.

Do not be victimized by your circumstances. Fight your way back from all these damaging and debilitating forces. Your life has a divine destiny. God, your Creator, has something planned just for you. He has a predetermined course for your life. But first, you must stop being desperate. A desperate person will try anything and they will fall for anything. The only One you should ever be desperate for is Jesus, because He is your strength.

Every woman should have what I refer to as the *stop agenda*. Stop trying to be what others want you to be, and be what God wants you to be. Stop trying to change your personality to suit people. Please God and allow Him to change you to suit His purpose and plan.

Stop barely surviving and get into the abundant life, which Jesus offers.

Stop telling yourself you cannot. God says you can.

Stop telling yourself that there is no hope; there is hope.

Stop saying it's over. God is saying a new beginning, a second chance, and a fresh start.

Stop falling apart. Simply allow God to take His position and place in your life.

Be wise women. God is waiting to set the plan He has for your life in motion. But first come out from under all that other stuff that is holding your progress and success in check. Sheer determination is not enough. God is our refuge and strength. He is our present help in times of turmoil. Learn to desire and expect God's best for your life. Go with His plan and His agenda. There are many things God wants to share with you concerning His plan for your life.

The harvest has past; the summer has ended, and many of you still do not know God's divine destiny for your life. In other words, your season of opportunity and productiveness came and went, and you did not even recognize that it was your time and your turn.

How easy it is to become satisfied with the status quo and a lifestyle of mediocrity. Get up, shake off that apathy and get out from under past failures and wasted years. Move away from yesterday and move into today. Yesterday serves only to teach us the intended lessons for today. Apply the lessons and get moving. Come out from under the "I can't syndrome," and get under the "I AM" truth of God.

Jesus is the great I AM and through Him, we can do all things. In His Name, come out from under the hurt and get under the healing, and come from under the pain and get under the plan. It is most necessary that you embrace God's plan for your life in order to attain your new beginning. Seeking to attain this new beginning before embracing His plan for your life is like putting the cart before the horse. You just won't get anywhere in life worthwhile.

Here you are, all ready to go, but making no progress because you are trying to attain your new beginning outside the divine plan of God. Not only that, but you are busy here and there, involved in a lot of activities, yet you are accomplishing very little because you are working your agenda instead of allowing God to work His agenda for your life. And once again, depression sets in because nothing seems to work out for you. No matter how hard you try, you can't seem to get past that wall that is blocking your progress.

Let me assure you, we all have our "Waterloo"—that one thing, or that one battle that leaves us feeling overwhelmingly defeated and drained. Don't you dare give up! There is a plan that is an asset and not a liability for your life. Also, there is a key that will unlock the door to your new beginning. Only God, however, has the key and only God knows what lock in your life the key fits. In other words, only God knows what needs to be pulled out of your life and what needs to be put in your life to attain your destiny. Apart from Him, we can do nothing successfully and apart from His plan, no other plan will work effectively.

Right now you may feel like your life is nothing but ashes, but do not despair. Take those ashes—the ashes of that broken heart, broken promises, broken relationship, and crushed hope, give them to God and ask Him to make them into something beautiful and worthwhile. Allow Him to do it His way, even when you do not understand what He is doing.

Now, for your divine destiny, you need divine persistence, endurance, and courage. You need a lasting steadiness and a firm hold on faith. In short, you need tenacity. There are obstacles and barriers preceding you, therefore, you will need endurance to forge full speed ahead. If you expect to last and reach your expected or predetermined end, you must be steady and godly aggressive.

Three places of testing will challenge you when you go after your divine destiny, and all three experiences are necessary in your life. You will have your Red Sea experience, your wilderness experience, and your Jordan experience.

First, you will be confronted by your Red Sea experience. During biblical times, if you located the Red Sea on a map, you would see that it was a sea "between" Egypt and Arabia. Egypt represents your circumstance and Arabia represents your deliverance or destiny. The Red Sea represents Satan, the defeatist.

Understand this, Satan stands between you and your destiny because he wants to keep you in the situation that you are in. He knows that in order for you to reach your destiny, you must cross your "Red Sea." Therefore, you are going to confront him, not just encounter him. Now, you have a decision to make. You can either choose to allow God to bring you through and out of that situation into your destiny, or you can choose to stay there and let Satan have your victory. If you want God to bring you out and through your Red Sea, surrender everything to Him. Even those things you count insignificant. Do not be afraid to give it all up to God. Allow Him to empower you so that you can confront the enemy in His more than power. You have to cross over to the other side, because Arabia, which represents your destiny, awaits you.

God has your Red Sea under control and has given you power over it, also. Jesus states emphatically in Luke 10:19, *"Behold, I give you power to tread on serpents and scorpions, and over all the power of the enemy: and nothing shall by any means hurt you."* That is the promise from Jesus, the One who possesses all power, so continue on your journey. You have everything you need in Him.

We find these words in Hebrews 11:29, *"By faith they passed through the Red Sea."* By faith they passed through and so must you. If you expect to get over to the other side to deliverance, you must trust God. Faith is your passport to get you where you need to go. Faith is not shaken by circumstances or problems. It does not tremble at what it sees and it is not unsteady. Nothing disturbs, shocks, or weakens grounded faith. Flesh is shaken by circumstances and trembles by what it sees, but not faith. Circumstances disturb, shock, and weaken our flesh, but not grounded faith. Faith sees nothing—grounded faith that is, that causes it to waver (See Psalms 62:1-2). Indeed, you might be shaken and shocked by your circumstances, but your grounded faith remains steady and unflinching.

Even though the Red Sea is your hard place, you can still walk through because God is with you. And your faith knows before God allows a situation to drown you, He will dry it up. So walk on through, keep moving, and continue progressing towards your destiny.

Next, comes your wilderness test or experience. This is where Satan engages you in a battle of the mind and will, as he did with Jesus (See Luke 4). It is during your wilderness test that Satan will try to convince you to choose him over God, his way over God's way, and his plan over God's plan. It is here that Satan will use different tactics to manipulate you into compromising the will and righteousness of God. His goal is to persuade you to take his word over the truth of God's Word. He desperately wants you to believe his lies instead of God's truth.

Do not fall for his tactics. Stay focused. God's plan for your life is at stake. One thing for sure, in your wilderness test, you will find out whether or not you are in this thing with God for life. Here is where you will make up your mind to go with God all the way, or bow to Satan. It will be either yes, Lord, and divine destiny, or yes, devil, and demonic devastation.

Finally, your "Jordan" test comes. Geographically, Jordan is the region that begins in Northern Palestine at the junction of four streams, and winds its way southward until it empties into the Dead Sea. Your spiritual Jordan is absolutely essential to your destiny. Deliverances, breakthroughs, victories, and successes come with Jordan. You will not see everything clearly that awaits you because Jordan has a tendency to be muddy. Do not worry about the muddiness that blankets your destiny. God knows your expected end (2 Kings 5:14).

Your Jordan represents an overflow of harvests in your life. This will be your exceeding abundantly above period. The things you have been waiting for so long will now come into your life. The noble desires of your heart, plus the blessings that God has held in protected custody for you will finally be yours. Fortunately for you, you are now mature and stable enough to manage them wisely, because your Red Sea and wilderness experiences have prepared you for this harvest of blessings.

While you are in Jordan, everything that comes against you will fail as long as you remain in the will of God. No weapon will prosper, therefore, during your period in Jordan, you will be able to stand firm against all demonic attacks until you are completely out of the situation. However, you just cannot stand by Jordan's banks, you must go in. In other words, there is a going through time. Remember, it is a "river testing place" that begins in one location and overflows into something else, or another location. For you, that something else is your destiny.

Also, Jordan is constantly flowing, that is why it has to empty or pour into something else. Therefore, you need to get mobilized. You must prepare yourself for active service, and it is a must that you keep going, and not stop or detour. Your blessings are waiting to pour into your life (See Joshua 3:14-17). Sometimes, to get from where you are to where you need to be, you will have to lose or let go of the very thing you want to hold on to. Also, you will have to cast away, or walk away from something and sometimes someone, if God directs you to do so.

Scripture adequately states it this way: *"A time to get, and a time to lose; a time to keep, and a time to cast away"* (Ecclesiastes 3:6). Do not be stubborn. Let go. God has something very definite and very special in mind for you. Do not lose out as Naaman almost did with his blessing.

"And Elisha sent a messenger unto him, saying, Go and wash in Jordan seven times, and thy flesh shall come again to thee, and thou shalt be clean.

But Naaman was wroth, and went away, and said, Behold, I thought, He will surely come out to me, and stand, and call on the name of the Lord his God, and strike his hand over the place, and recover the leper.

Are not Abana and Pharpar, rivers of Damascus, better than all the waters of Israel?

May I not wash in them, and be clean? So he turned and went away in a rage.

And his servants came near, and spake unto him, and said, My father, if the prophet had bid thee do some great thing, wouldest thou not have done it? How much rather then, when he saith to thee, Wash, and be clean?

Then he went down, and dipped himself seven times in Jordan, according to the saying of the man of God: and his flesh came again like unto the flesh of a little child, and he was clean" (2 Kings 5:10-14).

Do not forget what you just read. From time to time, you will need to strengthen yourself with this scripture. Why? Simply because your destiny will not always come the way you desire it to come. You can bring victory into your life by following God's plan, but you cannot design or demand the method by which it comes. The way, method, technique and timing will be God's choices. All you need to know is victory will come.

Presently, many of you are on the verge of spiritual collapse because in your estimation, you have been waiting on God for such a long time. Please, please, hold on! Help is on the way. All really is well. So, whatever you do, do not let go of the promises God has made to you. He is there for you. He sees your inner turmoil even though outwardly, you are trying to hide it. On the outside, you are all smiles, but within you are screaming.

Even while you are sitting in church your silent scream is piercing the ears of God. You feel like no one can hear that scream other than yourself. Fortunately, God hears it, also. Take courage, prayer and tears are not the only things that stir God. That silent scream stirs God, also. He is turning away your captivity even now. God does not want you enslaved anymore than you want to be enslaved.

Furthermore, God does not want you bound by external controls. Those things that keep you limited, confined and restricted from His divine plan for your life. He will deliver you and make you whole again. Just do not throw in the towel. God is the healer of body, mind, soul, and spirit; rather, He is the healer of spirit, soul, mind, and body. It starts from within.

Sh-h-h, listen. Do you hear it? "Yes, Jesus loves me, yes, Jesus loves me, oh yes, Jesus loves me, for [...]." It is well—do not scream anymore.

Lesson On Life

Hanani, one of my brethren came, he and certain men of Judah; and I asked them concerning the Jews that had escaped, which were left of the captivity, and concerning Jerusalem.

And they said unto me, The remnant that are left of the captivity there in the province are in great affliction and reproach: the wall of Jerusalem also is broken down, and the gates thereof are burning with fire.

And it came to pass, when I heard these words, that I sat down and wept, and mourned certain days, and fasted, and prayed before the God of heaven.
Nehemiah 1:2-4

Better Days Ahead

There are many things that can cause you to miss out on your divine destiny if you allow them to do so. Using wisdom, however, you can take the things that are being used against you as liabilities and use them as assets in your life.

When Nehemiah heard about the Jews in captivity and the broken wall of Jerusalem, he wept. He wept because his fellow Jews were living in a state of great affliction and reproach. Living in distress on a daily basis, their minds and spirits remained in a grievous state. They were being abused and disgraced by people around them.

This was not the destiny God had for their lives. Nehemiah knew this, and their plight grieved him to no end. Upon hearing the full report, he had great sorrow of heart. As a matter of fact, Nehemiah was grieving so deeply for his brethren, it was apparent on his face. Of course, king Artaxerxes noticed his sadness.

Allow me to point something out here. Nehemiah did not stay in that mode of sadness and grief. *"I sat down and wept, and mourned certain days,"* he says. He grieved for a while and then took care of business. Nehemiah strengthened himself through fasting and prayer. There is a lesson to be learned here, and that lesson is—always prepare yourself before taking actions. Notice the order of the things he did. He wept, mourned, fasted, and then he prayed. The emphasis is on the last two things he did. The torn down wall had to be rebuilt, and it was going to take courage and strength to get the job done. Nehemiah, in other words, did what he had to do to be successful in his work.

Ladies, sometimes your walls are going to get torn and broken down. I am referring to your walls of hope, faith, joy, self-esteem, and self-worth, as well as your wall of peace. Occasionally, you will find yourself in great affliction, mentally, emotionally, and sometimes even physically. Some of you are going to be abused and degraded, shamed and blamed, while pursuing your destiny.

If you need to cry like Nehemiah did, go ahead and cry. However, after you finish crying, again emulate Nehemiah, go into action and rebuild your wall. Through fasting, prayer, and the Word of God, rebuild those walls. You do not have to cry forever; get up and persevere.

"Weeping may endure for a night, but joy cometh in the morning" (Psalms 30:5). Good morning!!!

Lesson On Life

And therefore will the Lord wait, that He may be gracious unto you, and therefore will He be exalted, that He may have mercy upon you: for the Lord is a God of judgment: blessed are they that wait for Him.

For the people shall dwell in Zion at Jerusalem: thou shall weep no more: He shall be very gracious unto thee at the voice of thy cry; when He shall hear it, He will answer thee.

And though the Lord give you the bread of adversity, and the water of affliction, yet shall not thy teachers be removed into a corner anymore, but thine eyes shall see thy teachers:

And thine ears shall hear a word behind thee, saying, This is the way, walk ye in it....

Ye shall have a song, as in the night when a holy solemnity is kept; and gladness of heart, as when one goeth with a pipe to come into the mountain of the Lord, to the mighty One of Israel.

Isaiah 30:18-21a, 29

The Essence of True Womanhood

I Can, You Can, We Can

Granted, you have been through the storm and rain, the fire and flood, the valley and the desert; but whether you realize it or not, you are a better and more mature woman because of it. You are now ready to expand your hard earned knowledge on the true essence of womanhood. Looking back, you learned the value of trials and tribulations in your life, and the importance they played in getting you where you are today.

Having been enlightened by the many afflictions you have suffered, you now know that the essence of true womanhood is not about having a relationship with a man, necessarily. Neither is it about outer beauty or being sexy. The essence of true womanhood is the sum total of a woman. It is all the things that make that person what she is. Womanhood includes all the important elements and attributes that can be seen or felt. The essence of true womanhood is the heart, mind, will, soul, and spirit of a woman. It is about the total substance of being who and what she is in life.

Womanhood is about how we made it to where we are; the joy and the pain we encountered on our journey, and even the crises and challenges along the way. It is about knowing how to get back up after life has knocked us down. It is recognizing new opportunities and turning points, and knowing that even though our minds, bodies, hearts, and emotions at times can be vulnerable; ultimately, everything works for our highest good. Our learning experiences have taught us to take our lumps and losses while still keeping our eyes on the attainable prize.

The Essence of True Womanhood

The true essence of womanhood is about having a relationship with our Maker and Creator, first and foremost. It is about being open-minded while being single-minded and unrelenting in pursuing our divine destiny. Therefore, womanhood is to be woman from A-Z.

Ability-As women, we have the power and capacity to do great things.

Backbone-We have strength to endure and stand. We know how to function effectively under pressure when we resolve to do so. We do not crumble easily.

Charm-As women, we have captivating qualities. God not only made woman an attractive being, but a delightful one, also.

Diligent-We readily apply ourselves, giving earnest efforts to accomplish whatever needs accomplishing. We are persistent creatures.

Efficient-Women are competent, productive, skillful, and proficient. We use requisite knowledge intelligently to produce a desired effect.

Faith-A woman willingly puts her trust and confidence in others, which sometimes results in her getting hurt and deeply disappointed. Yet, we refuse to let go of our faith, because it is our faith that sees us through life's journey.

Growth-We believe in enhancing ourselves. We study to increase in knowledge, expand our horizons, and develop ourselves more fully in every area of our lives. We are constantly evolving by degrees to become better by attaining a greater maturity and understanding about ourselves.

Hope-Because we have high expectations for ourselves, we look forward to better things with confidence. We naturally expect and anticipate conditions to get better regardless of the situations we sometimes find ourselves in. We are known for being optimistic in the most pessimistic circumstances, because of the hope that is in us.

Ideal-Women believe in a certain standard of perfection and excellence. Visionaries by nature, we will take an intangible idea and make it a tangible reality. We are naturally gifted to take a concept and turn that concept into substance.

Judicious-Down through the centuries, women have always had a hand molding nations. From the home, to the school, to the office, and to the White House, what we have poured into others can be seen. Because of judicious women in their lives, men have been able to accomplish great feats. Thanks to women who used good judgment and made it a point to be well-advised and sensible, insecure little boys grew up to become well-established men. Our prudence and discretion pay off.

Kind-We have a gracious benevolent nature. We are accommodating, sympathetic and obliging. Unfortunately, because of these very traits, we get taken advantage of many times. Still, we are what we are.

Longsuffering-Possessing patient endurance, women will remain in abusive and stressful situations when they should have left long ago. Their visionary nature of hope kicks in and they endeavor to endure a while longer hoping, hoping, hoping.

Merciful-By character, women are also compassionate. When one finds a hard-hearted woman, just know that life has knocked her down so many times that she now resorts to using cruelness as a barrier to shield herself.

Nice-For the most part, a woman is pleasant to be around because she is caring, concerned, and tactful as she deals with others.

Observant-Alert, watchful, and attentive—that's woman for sure. She notices and discerns things that the opposite sex ordinarily would not see.

Peaceful-Wise women avoid strife and dissension. We like harmony in our environment and in our lives. Sometimes, we find ourselves adjusting to unfair situations for the sake of peace, simply because we enjoy tranquility.

Quality-Women are beings of distinction. Worthwhile and valuable, we have been given divine attributes that stand out wherever we are. God made woman to be a high caliber creature.

Responsible-Accountable and reliable, dependable and stable, we keep our homes together when the head of the home walks away or dies. Our children can rely on us because we obligate ourselves to doing that which is right and good.

Sincere-It is in a woman's heart—genuiness, that is. Women are open and straightforward, truthful and frank. We are very candid in our feelings, actions, words, and emotions. When a woman says or does something, usually, it is straight from the heart.

Trustworthy-Wise women know how to keep things confidential; we refuse to be talebearers or gossipers.

Useful-Helpful, handy, and resourceful, women are beneficial to have around. We understand that we have a purpose for living, and we serve that purpose by being productive in our homes, as well as in society.

Virtue-As beings of moral excellence, goodness, and integrity, wise women will not allow themselves to become corrupt. Neither will we corrupt others. We are decent, ethical, and honorable in the fashions we conduct ourselves in the affairs of life.

Well-Informed-Woman has an inner thirst for knowledge. She attains useful information and enlightenment, and she then makes sure that the information is reliable before she passes that knowledge on to others. She does her homework to keep from misleading anyone.

Xn-We live a Christ-centered life. He is our main focus and our first priority in every area of life. We have this understanding—without Christ, we are nothing, and accomplish nothing of any lasting value.

Yourself-Women should be themselves and stay with their own divinely given personality, and forget about impressing people. Just please God.

Zealous-Women need to be active and devoted to whatever God has called and anointed them to do. Be endeavourers in life. Always keep an enthusiastic mind and spirit, as much as possible.

Now you know why true womanhood is not to be diminished, but exalted. God gave woman her irreplaceable role and this role is not to be taken lightly. Woman has the ability to be many things because God created her with manifold capabilities. She can be a well, spring, or garden. A fountain, orchard, or door (See Solomon's Song 2:11).

Again, women are not without faults or flaws, imperfections or shortcomings, yet these things should not lessen or diminish our capabilities. When we maintain positive, godly attitudes, motivate and discipline ourselves on a day to day basis, we can achieve without measure. It is essential that we take responsibility for our actions, so make it a top priority to know and understand yourself.

Undoubtedly, there will be times in your life you will be faced with an ordeal and you will think to yourself—I cannot deal with this. Let me assure you of this one thing, you can. In the words of Eleanor Roosevelt, "You must do the thing you think you cannot do." Rise to the challenge. Have the "little red engine" attitude: I think I can, I think I can, I know I can. If the challenge is there in your life, you can deal with it successfully, otherwise, it would not be there.

God is able to do the impossible in your life, when you depend on Him. He can bring hope out of hopelessness, success out of failure, and purpose out of pain. Do not give in to thoughts of failure and defeat, and do not allow anything to shake or destroy your confidence in God.

Focus yourself. Your life does not have to be chaos and disorder because you are being faced with a new challenge.

Never forget, you have an enemy who will fight you every step of the way to keep you from your destiny. The adversary will ruffle your spirit and perturb your mind. He will disconcert and confuse you to keep you from becoming all that God created you to become. Keep this in mind: God has not given you the spirit of fear. Therefore, if you want to attain the purpose God has for your life, you must be strong, determined, and courageous.

It's breakthrough time! Time for some choice blessings, comfort, prosperity, and success in your life. Although God allowed the bread of adversity and the water of affliction into your life, still, He's waiting to be gracious to you. Your day has arrived! Yes, you have experienced many calamities and catastrophes, as well as disasters, hardships, and misfortunes, but God wants to alleviate those things for you. He wants to relieve you of the burdens, loads, and overloads you are carrying. You have been oppressed, troubled and taxed for too long. It is now time for some solace. God desires to soothe your wounds and pains.

God delights in giving out good things, therefore, He is looking forward to lessening your load, grief, and financial lack. He desires to be your mitigator. God wants to ease the severity and harshness of your distressful situation, and diminish its force and intensity in your life. He wants to extend more grace to you. Acting as divine Mitigator has become necessary because some have lost focus of their divine destiny.

Your situation, unfortunately, caused you agitation of the mind. It has caused mental and emotional disturbance for you. Your emotional well-being is at stake, and God wants to allay the situation. It is His desire to put to rest old issues in your life and to quiet your innerself. Once and for all, He is going to put to rest your tumult, fears, and suspicions.

Rise up ladies, a fresh harvest and new summer are on the horizon. The old hurts and pains have been healed and your health has been recovered. Emerge out of that shell you withdrew into. God has heard your prayers and turned away the things that were holding you captive. Get off the trail and get back on the path of your God-given destiny. Tranquility, peace, quietness, and calmness have been restored in your life. Your season of tears is over and your season for true happiness has returned.

Delight yourself in God's grace. Your walls have been rebuilt, and God's plan for your life is on the verge of being accomplished. Keep doing that "David thing" in your life, continue to encourage yourself in the Lord, your God. Keep striving, keep pressing, continue to endure as a good soldier. For she that continues will be delivered, so that she can attain her divine goal.

"... *For the Lord is a God of judgment: blessed are all they that wait for Him*" (Isaiah 30:18c). Do not get impatient. Dorothy Thompson states it so adequately: "Courage, it would seem, is nothing less than the power to overcome, while continuing to affirm inwardly that life with all its sorrows is good; that everything is meaningful even if in a sense beyond our understanding; and that there is always tomorrow."

Oh yes, take heart, you are a more than woman, not a rib. As you can see, the central theme throughout this book is "more than." As a woman representing the very best pertaining to womanhood, you must always walk in your God-given *more than* status. Always.

"*Being confident of this very thing, that He which hath begun a good work in you will perform it until the day of Jesus Christ*" (Philippians 1:6).

From My Heart To God's Ears

Lord, let every woman suffering from the less than syndrome realize they do not have to stay as they are. Let them know that there is a "more than power" available to them. Help them to become everything you created them to be in life. Let the oil of your Spirit purify and heal. In Jesus Name, Amen.

About the Author

Janie C. Williams resides in Selma, Alabama with her husband, Robert.

Mrs. Williams is a member of the Church of God in Christ, a licensed evangelist and president of the Young Women Christian Council.

The proud mother of three children—Renee, Robert Jr., and Regina, the fantastic three Rs. Mrs. Williams is also the proud, proud grandmother of Tyrenee Jeanae Nevith.

Notes

Notes

Notes

Notes

www.ingramcontent.com/pod-product-compliance
Lightning Source LLC
Chambersburg PA
CBHW071834290426
44109CB00017B/1821